YOU CAN GIVE AN ANSWER

You Can Give An Answer
© 2018 Steven A. Hein

Published by:
1517 Publishing
PO Box 54032
Irvine, CA 92619-4032

Printed in the United States of America

Cover design by Brenton Clarke Little

Publisher's Cataloging-In-Publication Data
(Prepared by The Donohue Group, Inc.)
Names: Hein, Steven A. (Steven Arthur), 1944–
Title: You can give an answer : a study in Christian apologetics / by Steven A. Hein.
Description: Irvine, CA : 1517 Publishing, [2018] | Includes discussion questions. | Includes bibliographical references.
Identifiers: ISBN 9781945500176 (softcover) | ISBN 1945500174 (softcover) | ISBN 9781945978074 (ebook) | ISBN 1945978074 (ebook)
Subjects: LCSH: Apologetics.
Classification: LCC BT1103 .H45 2018 (print) | LCC BT1103 (ebook) | DDC 239—dc23

YOU CAN GIVE AN ANSWER

A STUDY IN CHRISTIAN APOLOGETICS

◀ STEVEN HEIN ▶

FIFTEEN · SEVENTEEN PUBLISHING

1517.

Unit One

An Introduction to Apologetics

"What is faith?" asked the second-grade Sunday school teacher. Mike's little hand went up like a flash, and, having been called on by the teacher, he responded, "Believing something that you know isn't true."

Many non-Christians today would agree with Mike's definition. They often refuse to give the Christian faith an honest hearing because of the mistaken conviction that to become a Christian is to commit intellectual suicide. For them, Christianity is something akin to old-fashioned superstition and fantasy, whereas they live in the realm of the "real world," which deals with reason, evidence, and cold hard facts.

Tragically, many Christians also feel that a great gulf divides the realm of evidence and demonstrable truth from the central tenets of the Christian faith. Such a position often makes it difficult for Christians to make a forceful and compelling presentation of the Gospel to the non-Christian when intellectual reservations are raised and reasons for faith requested. Many a witnessing situation has been blunted by the inability or unwillingness of Christians to provide the non-Christian with compelling evidence for the truthfulness of the message of salvation that we proclaim.

In the New Testament, the Gospel of Jesus Christ is always equated with the truth. Truth is always the opposite of error. St. Paul identifies non-Christians as those who "do not obey the truth" (2 Thess. 2:11–12). Christians need to realize that if there is no way of objectively establishing what the truth is, such statements of St. Paul would be meaningless. As we carry out the great commission in our age, we must always demonstrate man's need of the Gospel by the accusing finger of the Law. Yet having done this, we must also demonstrate that the Good News of salvation through Christ is the only answer, not just because it works, but *because it is true*. How can this be accomplished?

A. What Is Apologetics?

It is the conviction of this study that *Christian apologetics* can be of great value to Christians as they witness to others about the saving Gospel of Jesus Christ. Whereas evangelism involves proclaiming and explaining the Gospel message that people might be saved, apologetics deals with defending the truthfulness of the Gospel when objections or challenges to the faith are raised. Negatively speaking, apologetics seeks to identify and remove intellectual obstacles that, in the non-Christian's mind, are precluding an honest consideration of the Christian faith. From the positive side, apologetics seeks to confront the non-Christian with compelling reasons and evidence that ground or give support to the truthfulness of Christianity. Apologetics also serves to calm honest and serious doubts or intellectual conflicts among believers (e.g., the Bible-science debate, creation vs. evolution).

Let's see what the Scriptures say about apologetics:

Read 1 Peter 3:14–15

1. What is Peter asking of you, the reader, in verse 15?
2. The word *defense* (RSV) is a translation of the Greek word *apologia*, from which we get the term *apologetics*. According to Peter, with what attitude is the apologetic task undertaken by Christians?
3. Discuss some ways in which Christians can follow the instruction of these two verses without engaging in harmful arguments?

It must be stressed that it is not an objective of apologetics to argue someone into the kingdom of God. Such a thing is really impossible. Saving faith is always the gift of the Holy Spirit, who works through our witness of the Gospel. Moreover, apologetics does not take upon itself the task of providing the nonbeliever *absolute objective certainty* concerning the truthfulness of the Christian faith. Certainty and heart-centered confidence is a gift of the Holy Spirit that follows from a saving faith relationship with Christ.

Rather, apologetics seeks to strip away the intellectual obstacles and smokescreens that many non-Christians often hide behind, so that they may forcefully and lovingly be confronted with the reality of their sinful condition and then God's glorious plan of salvation through Christ. Apologetics seeks to demonstrate and convince the nonbeliever that there is more evidence on behalf of the Christian truth claim than against. That is to say, for instance, that there is more evidence surrounding the life of Jesus that supports Peter's confession that He "is the Christ, the Son of the living God" (Matt. 16:16) than that He was but a mere human.

B. What Is the Relationship between Evidence and Faith?

In some circles today, faith is defined as "believing without evidence." This, however, is not the understanding of faith in the New Testament. Such a faith would be like a blind leap into the dark, and since one patch of darkness is no different from any other, such a faith would be devoid of significance and meaning. Moreover, a New Testament understanding of faith is not a blind human quest for truth but the direct consequence of what has been discovered about the identity of Jesus Christ and the purpose of His life, death, and resurrection.

The writer of the Epistle to the Hebrews described faith as "the assurance of things hoped for and the conviction of things not seen" (Heb. 11:1). As Christians, our hope certainly centers on Christ with a Spirit-produced conviction that in Him we have complete forgiveness and reconciliation with God and thus shall be partakers of the fullness of salvation. Let us look at a few passages of Scripture and discover on what basis such faith assurance and conviction rests. We will also examine the role that evidence plays in relation to faith.

Read 1 Corinthians 15:3–8, 13–20

1. What kind of relationship does Paul make between the fact of the resurrection of Christ and our trust in the forgiveness of sins, eternal life, and our own resurrection?
2. What kind of evidence does Paul offer the reader concerning the reality of Christ's resurrection?
3. What kind of status or importance does eyewitness testimony have in our society today (e.g., our judicial system)?

Read Acts 1:1–3; 2:22, 29–36
and Hebrews 2:3–4

1. What kind of "convincing proofs" (Acts 1:3) were presented by Christ to which the writer of Acts might be referring?
2. What kind of evidence does Peter offer (in Acts 2:22, 29–32) to the people that Jesus is the promised Messiah?
3. How has God confirmed for us the message of salvation that we have received from Christ and the apostles in the writings of the New Testament (Heb. 2:3–4)?
4. Discuss how these passages might affect the way in which we share the Gospel of Christ Jesus and exhort others to believe. What place should the use of factual evidence have in our appeals for belief?

Read John 20:30–31

1. What purpose does John have for the signs or miracles of Jesus that he reports in his gospel?

The above passages clearly show that the New Testament writers exhort the reader to make a response of faith to the person and work of Jesus

Christ. It is also clear, however, that they do so on the basis of compelling evidence that strongly supports the claims that Jesus is the risen Son of God and therefore the only one in whom we may have life and reconciliation with God. Faith is not commanded as a blind subjective leap; rather, it is on the basis of many signs and miracles that Jesus manifested and to which the apostles offer compelling eyewitness testimony.

Such events as the miracles of Christ and His bodily resurrection became a part of the proclamation of the Gospel by the apostles as they forcefully and effectively offered a defense of the hope that was within them (see especially Peter's sermon in Acts 2). We, as witnesses of Christ today, may utilize the same evidences that the apostles proclaimed, so that the Gospel may be proclaimed and defended in our day as successfully as it was in theirs. In our next lesson, we will explore more closely how apologetics was engaged in the ministries of our Lord and the apostles.

Unit Two

Observing Apologetics
in the New Testament

The necessity of providing a basis or grounding for the claims of the Christian faith is only real and important if it can be demonstrated that the ministry of Jesus and the apostles involved the task of apologetics. We must examine the way in which they proclaimed the Good News and the true identity of Jesus of Nazareth. Did they just announce these central aspects of Christianity, or did they also provide objective evidence to back up such claims? Let us look first at the way in which Jesus carried out His proclamation of the Gospel during His ministry.

A. Apologetics in the Ministry of Jesus

Read Matthew 9:1–8

1. Jesus asked the crowd, "Which is easier to say, 'Your sins are forgiven' or to say 'Rise and walk'?" If you were to answer His question, what would you say and why?
2. What purpose did Jesus have in mind when He spoke and acted in this incident? Did He accomplish that purpose?
3. What role did healing have for Jesus' ministry?

Certainly the Jewish crowd knew that only God could forgive sins. With Jesus implying that He had such divine power, the conclusion that Jesus was God was forced into the forefront for the crowd's consideration. There seemed to be only three major options from which the individuals in the crowd could choose. Jesus was a blaspheming liar (claiming to be God but knowingly was not), He was a raving lunatic (actually thinking He was God but was mistaken), or He truly did have power to forgive sins because He was, in fact, God incarnate. We know from verse 3 toward which option the scribes were leaning.

Notice how Jesus used the situation to provide an objective basis for the people to perceive the correct option on the identity issue. At the same time, He neutralized the effect of the skeptical scribes. Jesus recognized that His claim of power to forgive sins (and thus His identity with God) was not something that was directly demonstrable. He thus linked this extraordinary power that the people were unable to see to another equally unusual one—healing a man paralyzed from birth—that the people could see. In this way, Jesus effectively provided a visible basis for the people's faith that He had power to forgive sin, and He effectively defended Himself against those who sought to deny and discredit His divine identity.

Read Luke 3:18–20 and 7:18–23

1. What was the nature of John's problem?
2. How did Jesus answer John's question and calm his doubts?
3. What implications does Jesus' handling of John's doubts have for our ministry to other Christians who are plagued with doubts?

Read John 10:30–39

1. What is the real problem of Jesus' hearers?

2. How does Jesus offer to help them? Compare this with the above cited ministry to John the Baptist.

3. What implications does the outcome of this incident have upon expectations of our own efforts of defending the Gospel?

Read John 20:19–29

1. What was Thomas's problem and why do you think he had one? What kind of evidence did he refuse to be swayed by?

2. How did Jesus minister to the intellectual reservations of Thomas? What was the effect?

3. What did Jesus mean (in verse 29) when He said, "Blessed are those who have not seen and yet believe"?

In each of the above occasions, we see how our Lord witnessed to those who had doubts and reservations that stood in the way of a confident acceptance of Jesus as divine Savior. In each case, He sought to remove obstacles to faith by providing compelling reasons and objective evidence that gave powerful support to His true identity.

In ministering to John the Baptist and his doubts regarding whether Jesus was the promised Messiah, our Lord did not simply instruct John's disciples to urge John to delve deeper into his own religious experience. He rather pointed to works that John could see unmistakably belonged to the promised Messiah ("The blind receive their sight, the lame walk, the lepers are cleansed, and the deaf hear, the dead are raised up, the poor have the Good News preached to them" [Luke 7:22]).

From the above reading in John 10, we see that our Lord was not always successful in overcoming unbelief, even when compelling reasons and evidence for faith were presented. This incident serves well to emphasize the point that no one can be coerced into belief or forced into a saving faith relationship with Christ. Apologetics may show that there is more evidence on the side of faith and Christ's divine identity than against it, but there is always the possibility of stubborn unbelief.

The problem, however, is not with the evidence that Jesus has provided as to His true identity. Rather, the problem is with sinful man's will, which wants nothing to do with God and His plan of salvation and hence often resists the direction toward which the evidence would lead. If apologetics can help the non-Christian to see that the real reasons for his unbelief involve a desire to live life apart from the forgiveness and Lordship of Christ and not because of some supposed offense to the intellect, then it will have accomplished a great deal.

In our familiar reading from John 20 concerning Christ's appearance to Thomas, we see how persuasion concerning Christ's resurrection was used by the Holy Spirit to bring about a personal faith in Jesus as Lord and God. Why is it that we often refer to him as "doubting Thomas"? What did Thomas doubt? Many Christians have taken Jesus' words "Blessed are those who have not seen and yet believe" (John 20:29) to mean something like the following: "Thomas, you have demanded some form of evidence to give objective support to your faith commitment; blessed are those who believe on the basis of no objective foundation of evidence at all"!

Is this really what Jesus is saying? We think of Thomas as a skeptic, and so he was. But what was the true nature of his skepticism? Perhaps verse 25 gives us the clue. All the disciples, with the exception of Thomas, had seen the risen Lord. Thomas had the benefit of seemingly overwhelming evidence that Christ had risen from the dead on the basis of corroborating eyewitness testimony of his closest friends. And yet, even in the face of this, he would not believe.

Think about the importance that has always been given to corroborated eyewitness testimony. Our whole court system is built upon such a basis. The fate of all who are charged with crimes is determined largely on the basis of a reconstruction of what happened through evidence from eyewitness testimony. To be skeptical of this kind of evidence is to have virtually all history removed from the sphere of knowledge! We could know very little of the past.

Jesus understood the strength and sufficiency of eyewitness testimony. Thomas, however, wanted more—he demanded direct personal contact with the risen Lord. Jesus' words therefore can best be understood to mean, "Blessed are those who rest their faith commitment in the sufficiency of eyewitness testimony." This is the kind of testimony that the Scriptures invite us to share as we confront others with the personal testimony of the apostles, those who saw and believed.

Notice how the apostles witnessed to Christ with their eyewitness testimony.

B. Apologetics in the Ministry of the Apostles

Read 2 Peter 1:13–21

1. On what basis does Peter ask for a hearing of the Gospel in verses 16–18?
2. What event is alluded to by Peter?

Read Acts 26:1–29

1. What was Paul's goal in speaking to King Agrippa?
2. To what does Paul appeal in verse 26?

Read 1 John 1:1–4

1. What are the kinds of testimony that John offers concerning Jesus?

Certainly the eyewitness quality of evidence was very important to our Lord in the fulfilling of the great commission. Indeed, it was a requirement that an apostle be an eyewitness of the risen Lord (Acts 1:21–22). Through the apostolic witness in the New Testament, we have powerful evidences of Christ's Lordship and divine identity. His miracles, fulfillment of prophecy, and His resurrection have all been offered by Christ in support of His Divine Lordship and mission. We can share them in our witnessing to others—and on the basis of eyewitness testimony!

Unit Three

Dealing with Objections

A prominent reason that many sincere and dedicated Christians tend to shy away from personal witnessing of the Gospel is the fear of either being asked a question whose answer they do not know or being faced with a critical objection to the Christian faith that they cannot handle. Rather than face what is thought to be a terrible and humiliating embarrassment of the first order, many Christians opt out of the opportunities and joys of personal evangelism.

It is certainly true that effective witnessing demands that we obtain knowledge and skill in clearly communicating the key aspects of our faith in Christ to those who have not heard.

Nevertheless, we need not fear the occasional question or challenge that may be raised in the context of our witness. Such situations provide real opportunities to strengthen our claim that the Gospel is to be believed precisely because it is true. As we have seen in the last two units, Christ and the apostles have provided us with many reasons and evidences that give support to the key salvation events and the true mission and identity of Christ.

Fears that every non-Christian is a "walking encyclopedia" full of extremely complex and sophisticated objections to the Christian faith are really unfounded. Actually, objections tend to be rather limited in number and are capable of being handled by the Christian who has done a modest amount of preparation in anticipation of them.

Our purpose in this unit is to discuss two of the more popular objections or sticky challenges that are often raised by non-Christians in our society and to explore some ways in which they might effectively be dealt with in the context of a personal witnessing situation.

A. Miracles

Often the objection is raised in one form or another that Christianity simply cannot be true because the miraculous events that the faith proclaims (e.g., resurrections from the dead, restoring sight to the blind, changing water to wine) have been proven impossible or highly suspect by modern science. Those who offer this objection often attempt to explain away Biblical testimony to the occurrence of miracles by charging that men such as the followers of Christ naively believed that supernatural miracles were common realities. They lived in a prescientific age that knew nothing of the laws of nature. "Miracles were the only way that many things could be explained back then," or so the story goes. Let's examine how such an objection might be handled.

Read Matthew 1:18-21

1. What was Joseph's conclusion about Mary's pregnancy?
2. Does Joseph seem to have an understanding of human reproduction different from our modem understanding?

Read Matthew 8:23-27

1. What kind of reaction did the disciples display?

2. Does it seem that they reacted as though miracles were "usual" events or common interpretations?

Examples such as these could be multiplied. A close look at the way Biblical figures reacted to supernatural events simply does not reflect the allegation that miracles back then were "common realities" or usual explanations for what are now considered purely "natural" phenomena. Jesus' miracles usually elicited reactions of amazement, fear, misunderstanding, or even skeptical disbelief (as with Thomas, for instance).

Since the Enlightenment (eighteenth century), however, many non-Christian intellectuals have popularized the idea that miraculous events are rather unscientific notions. They have held a skeptical attitude about supernaturally caused events (as those recorded in Scripture), claiming that such interpretations must be considered the least probable of all possible explanations of a given event. They will accept the most improbable "natural" explanation rather than say that a miracle has occurred. Such a position has been based on an understanding of the universe as governed by "laws of nature," which have been established by uniform experience. By such laws, it is believed that most events in the world can sooner or later be explained. Miracles are looked upon as "violations" of the laws of nature, and since uniform experience has established these laws, there must be uniform experience, practically speaking, against their violation.

How can we as Christians respond to someone who holds such a position? First of all, we must recognize that the question "Do miracles occur?" is really another way of asking the question "Is there uniform experience of nature according to natural law?" Many critics of miracles, following the lead of the famous philosopher David Hume, simply assume the answer of yes to the latter question and use it in a circular argument to answer no to the question "Do miracles occur?" In his work *Miracles*, C. S. Lewis has rightly observed that we only know that there is uniform experience in the favor of natural law if we know that all reports concerning miracles are false. And we only know for sure that all reports of their occurrence are false if we know in advance that natural law has been established by uniform experience. We are arguing in a circle!

As Christians, we must help the non-Christian to see that the only way one can determine if miracles can occur is to investigate whether in fact one has occurred. Modern science today does not understand laws of nature to be *prescriptive* principles, as it once did, which govern how events must occur. Rather, they are seen simply as *descriptive* of how things usually appear to operate or happen in the physical world. Christians need to help the questioning unbeliever to see that modern science has not ruled out the possibility of miracles. Help can also be given so that the unbeliever recognizes that the Scriptures present impressive evidence that a very real God has been supernaturally active and has manifested Himself "by many signs and wonders."

B. The Problem of Evil

One of the most pressing questions that often is raised in the context of personal witnessing is "Why does God allow suffering and evil?" Some non-Christians would want to challenge the existence of the God of Biblical revelation by insisting that either God is all powerful but not all good and therefore does not put a stop to evil or He is all good but not all powerful and hence is unable to do anything about the problem.

Read Genesis 1:26–31, Romans 5:12–14, and Psalm 53:1–3

1. What does the Genesis passage tell us about God's original work in creation and the nature of man?
2. From the Romans and the Psalms passages, what truths can we relate concerning the origin, extent, and responsibility for evil in the world?

We must never forget that when God created the world and man as the crown of creation, He created them perfect—holy and blameless. Evil was not a part of His original creation, nor did He bring it into the world. To blame God for the world's present corrupted condition is about as fair as blaming the architect for the condition of a house gutted by fire at the hands of an arsonist! The Scriptures are very clear. Sin and evil entered the world through the disobedience of man, and because of that, death and all forms of human misery and suffering have been the consequence. Man is responsible for sin, not God!

But some have asked, "Could not God have made us so that we would not be able to sin?" We must respond by saying, "Yes, God could have, but then He would not have created human beings with wills of their own but puppets or machines." Consider any virtue of which a person is capable: love, kindness, honesty, faithfulness, or any of the virtues that Paul identified in Galatians 5. What are the natures of love in particular, for example, and virtue in general? In order for real love and virtue to exist, there must be freedom. Love is volitional in nature. Introduce force or coercion into the picture, and love becomes impossible.

God could have made us like puppets so that He would only have to pull the proper strings to have us go through all the outward manifestations of love and every other virtue in which He delights. It would not, however, be real love or real virtue as Paul describes in Galatians 5. God created us with freedom and independent wills because, being a God of love, He desired creatures who would be capable of returning His love with a love of our own. God's plan for man to respond with true love involved the built-in risk of man not loving at all but rather rebelling against God's love and rule. And we know from Scripture that the choice of rebellion was taken by our first parents and the resulting evil nature has been passed on to all generations.

The additional question is often raised, "But why doesn't God remove all evil from His creation now?" This is certainly something He could do. If God were to do so, He would do a complete job. But if God were to cleanse the entire universe of evil today, which of us would be around tomorrow? Many who would wish God to remove evil from the world right now think only of the evil "out there" and not about the evil that lies within their own hearts and lives. We must help the non-Christian, through the use of God's Law, see that "all have sinned and fall short of the glory of God" (Rom. 3:23) and therefore the presence of evil has infected his or her own thoughts, actions, values, and priorities.

Our most joyous message, however, is that God has done something about the problem of evil. In a most dramatic and costly manner, He dealt evil the most effective blow possible by sending His Son into the world to die for the sins of an evil-infected mankind. God is not soft on evil! Because of His good and righteous nature, all sin and evil must be punished. Yet through Christ and His death for sin, we may escape the ultimate judgment on evil and receive the power to begin to realize in our lives the love and virtues for which we were originally created.

Evil can be forgiven and ultimately conquered and banished in our lives through a relationship with Christ. God has conquered evil *for us* and has set a time limit for its presence in our lives and in the world. When Christ returns again, time will be up on sin and evil in the world. In that day for those who are in Christ, "they shall hunger no more, neither thirst anymore; the sun shall not strike them nor any scorching heat. For the Lamb in the midst of the throne will be their Shepherd and He will guide them to springs of living water; and God will wipe away every tear from their eyes" (Rev. 7:16–17).

Unit Four

Who Is Jesus?

It is difficult for us to know for sure whether God exists and what His attitude is toward us unless He takes the initiative and reveals Himself Are there any clues that history offers us concerning a possible revelation of God? Christians know of one big clue! In a relatively obscure village in Palestine, some two thousand years ago, a child was born in a stable. He was an unusual child who settled with His parents in Nazareth. When He was twelve, He amazed the Bible scholars in Jerusalem with His knowledge, and when rebuked for not having departed with His parents, He made the following strange reply: "Did you not know that I must be in My Father's house?" (Luke 2:49).

This one, Jesus of Nazareth, lived in obscurity until He was about thirty years of age, when He began a public ministry that lasted three years. He was kind and gentle, but unlike the religious teachers of His time, He taught "as one who had authority" (Matt. 7:29). The big question that He put to His closest followers was "Who do you say that I am?" When one of His followers replied, "You are the Christ, the Son of the living God" (Matt. 16:15–16), He was not shocked by the reply, nor did He rebuke the follower. Amazingly, He commended him!

On many other occasions, Jesus actually made this same claim Himself. On one occasion He said, "I and the Father are one." In response, the Jews wanted to stone Him for blasphemy "because you, being a man, make yourself God" (John 10:30–33). Jesus continually made the closest of connections with God. As John Stott has observed, "So close was His connection with God that He equated a man's attitude to Himself with the man's attitude to God. Thus, to know Him was to know God (John 8:19, 14:7). To see Him was to see God (12:45, 14:9). To believe in Him was to believe in God (1 2:44, 14:1). To receive Him was to receive God (Mark 9:37). To hate Him was to hate God (John 15:23). And to honor Him was to honor God (5:23)."

To the question in this unit title, "Who Is Jesus?," Christians have responded as did Peter. Jesus is "the Christ, the Son of the living God" (Matt. 16:16) and thus, like Thomas, have personally put their faith in Him as "my Lord and my God" (John 20:28). As we Christians witness to our faith to unbelievers, we must invite them to face the claims of Christ and personally answer for themselves, "Who is Jesus?"

Actually, there are only four possibilities. He was a liar, a lunatic, a legend, or the Son of God. If we believe that Jesus is not the Son of God, we are automatically affirming one of the other three alternatives. When those to whom we witness take this position, we should invite them to show us what evidence they have to back up their position. Let us briefly consider these alternatives.

A. Alternative One: Jesus Lied When He Said He Was God Incarnate

This possibility asserts that Jesus knew He was not God, but that He deliberately deceived His followers and those who listened to His teaching. Very few have seriously entertained this position. Most who would deny the divine identity of

Jesus nevertheless wish to acknowledge the high moral qualities of His personal life and teachings. Yet if Jesus lied so brazenly about the most central aspect of His teachings—that is, His own identity—He can hardly be considered a great moral example!

We must further inquire of those who would still wish to assert this position, "Do you have any evidence (beyond the issue at hand) that Jesus was a liar?" Or if Jesus' identity was the only lie, what was His motive for claiming to be God if He really was not?

Could Jesus have thought such a lie would bring Him material wealth and popularity?

Read Luke 9:57-58, 12:13-34,
22:66-71, and 23:13-25

Could Jesus, who was a Jew, have thought that such a lie would bring Him spiritual rewards?

Read Exodus 20:1-7, Deuteronomy
13:1-5, and Matthew 5:17-19

In dealing with non-Christians who might seriously entertain the view that Jesus lied concerning His divine identity, we must remind them that

such an act would be blasphemy of the highest
sort, which, for the Jew, was the most horren-
dous of all possible sins according to Mosaic Law.
Clearly such a lie, if it was one, would incur divine
condemnation, not spiritual rewards, on the very
basis of the moral law of the Old Testament, which
Jesus upheld to the fullest possible extent. Clearly
one is at a loss to find any reasonable motive for
Jesus to have knowledgeably lied concerning His
identity as God incarnate!

B. Alternative Two: Jesus Was a Lunatic; He Thought He Was God Incarnate but Was Deranged and Self-Deceived concerning His Own Identity

This bizarre idea simply does not accord with
the personality of Jesus that we so vividly see
in the gospel accounts. There we see no evidence
of the abnormality and imbalance that is charac-
teristic of derangement. Even under the extreme
pressures of the trials before the Sanhedrin, Herod,
and Pilate when His life was at stake, Jesus was
calm and serene. As C. S. Lewis so aptly observed,
"The discrepancy between the depth and sanity of
His moral teaching and the rampant megalomania

which must lie behind His theological teaching unless He is indeed God has never been satisfactorily got over."

The psychiatrist J. T. Fisher holds that if one were to boil down all the meat of the sum total of all authoritative articles on mental hygiene by the most qualified psychologists, the result would be a rough outline of the Sermon on the Mount. The position of derangement simply will not hold up psychologically. If Jesus' teachings provide a blueprint for optimum mental health, He cannot be a lunatic who totally misunderstands the nature of His own personality. Again, we must appeal to the nonbeliever who holds this view to show us his or her evidence.

C. Alternative Three: Jesus Is a Legend

This position, which some have held, maintains that Jesus of Nazareth never made the claim to be God incarnate, but that His followers deified Him, putting back into His mouth such claims in their preaching and writing after His death. In other words, Jesus' disciples were liars in their central teaching that Jesus was the Son of God, and thus they manufactured a legend.

This third alternative has several striking weaknesses. First of all, it has been shown conclusively that the four gospel accounts of Jesus' life and ministry were written within the lifetime of contemporaries of Christ. The world-famous archaeologist Dr. William F. Allbright has said that there is no reason to believe that any of the gospels were written later than 70 AD, within forty years of Jesus' death. For a legend in gospel form recording Christ's divine claims and authority to have gained such wide circulation and acceptance without a firm basis in fact is incredible! It would be as fantastic as someone in our time writing a biography of Franklin D. Roosevelt in which Roosevelt claimed to be God, to have power to forgive sins, and that he would rise from the dead. Such a wild story would neither gain acceptance nor be printed, because there are too many people around who knew Roosevelt and could easily refute the legendary errors.

Moreover, those who would seriously entertain the legend alternative need to be confronted with the question "Why was Jesus crucified?" The historical record of the gospels makes it clear that the Jewish leaders of the Sanhedrin were convinced that Jesus was guilty of blasphemy for claiming divine authority and identity (Mark

14:60–65 and John 19:1–11). On this basis, they delivered Him over to Pilate to be killed. Pilate, however, could not find any guilt according to civil law, yet handed Him over to be crucified at the urging of the crowd (see John 19:12–22).

If it were true that Jesus made no claims to be the Messiah, the Son of God, and the One who has authority to forgive sins, then we are faced with the following question: Why did the Jewish leaders urge Jesus' death? There does not seem to be any other answer to this question short of recognizing that Jesus Himself, not simply His disciples, proclaimed His divine identity.

Non-Christians also need to realize that all types of Jewish messianic speculation at the time were at variance with the messianic picture Jesus painted of Himself. Most of these portraits involved a strong political figure who would mobilize the Jewish people, throw off the Roman domination of Israel, and usher in an age of peace and prosperity as in the days of David and Solomon. Jesus' role as Suffering Servant who came to die for the sins of the world (Isa. 52:13–53:6) and whose kingdom is not of this world (John 18:36) simply did not fit the personal expectations that many had for the Messiah.

D. Alternative Four: Jesus Is the Son of God

It is not enough simply to demonstrate that there is little evidence for the above three alternatives in helping the nonbeliever come to grips with the identity of Jesus of Nazareth. Throughout much of life, talk is cheap. Jesus is not the only person in history to have claimed deity. Recently, Father Divine of Philadelphia claimed to be God. Because of very poor credentials to back up that claim, Father Divine is now both dead and largely forgotten. We as Christians need to show those to whom we witness that the credentials that Jesus presented on behalf of His claim of deity are impressive.

According to the eyewitness testimony offered to us in the gospels, Jesus demonstrated a power over the forces of nature as no mere human has ever exhibited—power that could only belong to the Creator of these forces. He calmed a raging storm of wind and waves on the Sea of Galilee to the utter amazement of His disciples. He fed five thousand people with a few fish and a couple of loaves of bread, turned water into wine at a marriage feast, and gave back to a grieving widow her son by raising him from the dead. Jesus not only demonstrated a loving concern for the sick and the crippled but also displayed the Creator's power. At His command, the blind could see, the deaf could hear, the paralyzed could walk, and the diseased were cured. Even His enemies could not refute His miraculous works. Rather they plotted to kill Him. "If we let Him go on thus," they said, "everyone will believe in Him" (John 11:48).

Jesus' enemies made good on their threat, but this only served to set the stage for the ultimate sign that Christ would offer to exhibit His true divine identity. This ultimate sign was His resurrection from the dead (Matt. 12:38–40).

When Jesus was crucified in Jerusalem, the city was filled with people who had come to celebrate the Jewish Passover. Because of the legal proceedings before Pilate and the mobs, the general public was well aware of what was transpiring. Because of Jesus' prediction that He would rise from the dead after three days as proof of His divinity, the Jewish religious leaders set a guard at Jesus' tomb to prevent the body from being stolen. Yet according to eyewitness testimony, Jesus did rise from the dead and was seen again and again over a forty-day period. These appearances are recorded with great detail (Luke 24:36–43; John 20:25–31).

Attempts have been made to explain the resurrection accounts naturalistically. Some have suggested that Jesus just fainted on the cross and revived in the cool of the tomb. Others, such as Hugh Schonfield in his *Passover Plot*, put forth the explanation that Jesus was given a drug that made Him seem to be dead, but in fact He was not. Some explanations such as these require a tremendous leap of faith, for they are completely out of line with the historical details that surround Jesus' life and the occasion of His death. Jesus surely died on the cross; the Roman crucifixion teams knew their business all too well! John explicitly tells us in his gospel that when a Roman soldier pierced Jesus' side with a spear, blood and water came out (John 19:34). This can only happen if a person is already dead.

Other critics, however, agree that Jesus did die and was buried, but they maintain that the body was stolen (see Matt. 27:62–66, 28:11–15). In response we must ask, "Who would have taken it?" Certainly it would not have been the Roman or Jewish parties, for they wanted to put down the followers of Jesus at all costs. That is why Jesus was crucified in the first place and why the guard at the tomb was set. What about the followers of Jesus? Could they have stolen the body? It is difficult to imagine a few cowardly fishermen, as the disciples were after the arrest of Jesus, overpowering Roman soldiers who were guarding the tomb, rolling away the great stone, and then beginning to tell a bizarre lie that Jesus was risen—and going to their deaths preaching the same story throughout the world! Such a story would be more astounding, if true, than the resurrection itself. To those who would seriously entertain such a theory, we must ask them to present their historical evidence to back up such an interpretation. We as Christians must boldly assert that we offer eyewitness testimony to back up our belief that Christ *was* truly raised from the dead and then ask for an evaluation of the quality of evidence that each position would offer.

If Christ did conquer the most basic of human problems—death itself—then it would be well to take His claims seriously and act upon them. We must confess with another skeptic, Thomas, that He who died and rose did so on our behalf, and thus He is "my Lord and my God."

In a world of increasing unbelief, we as witnessing Christians must make bold the claims of Christ, the evidences He has offered to us to back them up, and man's desperate need for a Lord and Savior. The evidences that challenge the unbeliever are ultimately from God and His Word. Through their proclamation and defense, we faithfully give an adequate answer and "defense for the hope that is in us" and provide the means for the Holy Spirit to bring people to faith in Christ as Lord and Savior.

CPSIA information can be obtained
at www.ICGtesting.com
Printed in the USA
JSHW031022090520
5507JS00003B/38

9 781945 500176